AN ISLAND SANCTUARY

AN ISLAND SANCTUARY

A HOUSE IN GREECE BY

John Stefanidis

JOHN STEFANIDIS AND SUSANNA MOORE
Principal photography by Fritz von der Schulenberg

RIZZOLI
NEW YORK

New York · Paris · London · Milan

CONTENTS

CAPTIONS BY JOHN STEFANIDIS

PREAMBLE

BY JOHN STEFANIDIS

T HERE COMES A TIME IN LIFE when you assess the friendships that have given you the most pleasure, amusement, and affection. The same can be said of a place or a house. In my lifetime, it is a house and a garden on the island of Patmos, Greece, that have nurtured the soul.

My house is a labyrinth on two floors. A typical example of *rus in urbe*, it sits firmly among its whitewashed neighbors, the walls of a fortress monastery above, houses to the left, right, and back, terraces cascading to the olive groves below.

There is not a window in the house without a heart-stopping view of luminous white houses; a chapel perched on the highest point of the island, dedicated to the Prophet Elijah; dry stone walls; small churches with rounded tops; the grandeur of the great monastery of St. John. Beyond the cubist composition of roofs sit two other places of God, the Convent of Evangelisimos and the Convent Zoodochos Pighi (Source of Life). And everywhere is the sea — steel blue, azure, turquoise, deepest sapphire, depending on the direction of the wind. On a still day, when the sea is calm, it is the color of mother-of-pearl with streaks of aquamarine; or cobalt with galloping white horses on the days the *meltemi* is blowing.

Goats graze on the hillsides, and in the evening the stillness is broken by the sound of their bells. The spiritual world of Byzantium is all around you. Church bells ring and the hum of early Christian chants, part of the Orthodox liturgy, floats across the fields, even as the ancient gods, always present in Greece, hover above you — Elijah's chapel is, after all, built on the site of a temple to Apollo. In the olive groves at the foot of the garden, Julian the Apostate still murmurs admonishments to return to the old ways.

IONIC (ΙΩΝΙΚΟΝ)

Because we have broken their statues,

Because we have turned them out of their temples,

They have not died, the gods, for that, at all.

O Land of Ionia, you, they love you still,

And you they still remember in their souls.

When an August morning dawns over you

Through your atmosphere passes an ardour from their life;

And sometimes an aerial youthful form,

Indefinite, with swift transition,

Passes upon your hills.

C. P. CAVAFY (Translated by Evangelos Sachperoglous)

8   If all this were not enough, there is the solace of a shady garden, with cypress, citrus, and pomegranate trees, rosemary, verbena, oregano, basil, and bay. There is the sound of birdsong, the fluttering of doves' wings and swallows nesting, and, on a calm day, the sonorous sound of the sea — waves breaking and retreating — can be heard through the whisper of pines.

There is something most satisfying in having cisterns to preserve water (the largest of which is in the courtyard entrance to the house); floor tiles that have been made in the same way for centuries; thick, white walls; doors and windows left ajar with the scent of jasmine, lemon, and orange blossom wafting from the terraces that descend steeply to the garden rooms, dovecote, and chapel.

Secluded on this most fortunate of islands, you gaze across the sparkling Aegean Sea to a galaxy of legendary isles: Samos and Ikaria to the north, Leros and Kos to the southeast, Astipalea and Amorgos to the southwest. Crete, birthplace of Artemis, lies to the south, and, farther still, the shores of Africa. North and east are the Greek and Roman ruins of Anatolia and, beyond, the Turkish plains where storks perch on rooftops — on and on, stretching to the immensity of the Asian steppes.

THE MYSTERIOUS ISLAND of Chilomodi with white cliffs, a black pebble beach, and one lone chapel.

The mind wanders to:

. . . I am Alpha and Omega, the first and the last: and, What thou seest,

write in a book, and send it unto the seven churches which are in Asia; unto Ephesus,

and unto Smyrna, and unto Pergamos, and unto Thyatira, and unto Sardis,

and unto Philadelphia, and unto Laodicea.

REVELATION OF ST. JOHN THE DIVINE [1.REV 1.8]

In an island sanctuary such as this, *mal du siècle* is kept at bay. The ethereal light, the countless shooting stars, the rising of the moon induce one to take Cavafy's schoolmasterly advice seriously:

AS BEST YOU CAN (ΟΣΟ ΜΠΟΡΕΙΣ)

Even if you cannot make your life the way you want,

try this, at least,

as best you can: do not demean it

by too much contact with the crowd

by too much movement and idle talk.

Do not demean it by dragging it along,

by wandering all the time and exposing it

to the daily foolishness

of social relations and encounters,

until it becomes an importunate stranger.

C.P. CAVAFY (Translated by Evangelos Sachperoglous)

On this island that refreshes the soul and arouses the senses, the charmed moments of halcyon days — laughter and contemplation — are evoked; sensations nowhere better expressed than by Odysseas Elytis:

11

WHAT ONE LOVES: AEGEODROME (ΑΙΓΑΙΟΔΡΟΜΟ)

When I opened my guidebook I understood. No maps or anything.

Just words. But words leading precisely to what I searched for. And

Slowly, turning the pages, I saw space being shaped like a tear by deep

emotion. And I inside.

agape	cardinal	eucalyptus	hedge	luff	oven	sails	such
Alexandra	castle	exile	heliotrope	mad	ozier	St. Anargyri	sun
All Soul's Day	caulking	fair	high ceiling	magic	pail	St. Mamas	swallow
anchor	cemetery	fallen leaves	high sea	Mall	PalmWeek	St. Monica	swordfish
anemone	chameleon	farmer cheese	holy water	mandarin	pampas	St. Paraskevi	tassel
Anna	chamomile	fern	honeysuckle	Mando	parapet	salt	Taxiarch
ant	chapel	feta	horse of the	marble	pass	salutations	tent
arch	chicken soup	fiancée	Virgin	Marina	pebble	sandstone	terraced
arm in arm	cicada	fig	hurricane	marzipan	pelago	schooner	three-masted
armoire	cistern	filter	hyacinth	mast	perch	scorpion	threshing
aspen	citrus	firefly	hydrangea	mastic	perpendicular	sea	ground
astringent	Claire	fireplace	hyssop	mat	petal	seabird	tiller
August	clear sailing	fisherman	icon	medusa	pew	sea breeze	tillia
bait	cliffs	fishhook	incense	melon	philodendron	sea cave	tomato
barbette	clockwork	fishing lights	Indian fig	memorial	phylactery	seafloor	turpentine
barrel	cobblestone	fishing line	isthmus	mint	pine	seal	turtledove
basil	colored pebbles	fishing net	ivy	mistral	pine resin	sea urchin	unspoken water
basket	comb	fish soup	jar	monastery	pinna	seaweed	vessel
bay leaf	cool wind	flag	jasmine	moon	pistachio	seine	veteran
beach	cork	flashlight	jib	mooring	pitch	September	vine leaves
beam-reach	cove	florins	jujube	morning joy	pitcher	sesame	vines
beeswax	crab	flowerpot	July	moss	plane tree	shack	vineyard
bell	cricket	flower water	jumping-jacks	motorboat	Pleiades	sheepskin	viper
bergamot	crops	foam	June	muleteer	plum	shell	virgin
birdsong	cross	fortune telling	keel	mullet	poppy	shrimp	wash
bitter sea	cuttlefish	fountain	kerchief	Muscat	port	shroud	watermelon
blanket	cyclamen	frankincense	kilns	must	prime	silvered	watersquash
bluefish	cypress	frapped	kiss	myrrh	promise	sirocco	wave
bluefly	dandelion	fresh	lament	Myrtle	prow	sister	weed
blueing	daphne	Froso	lampblack	naranja	psalter	sleep	well water
boat	deckhand	frost	lapping	nettles	pumice	slip	Westerly
bolt	desert island	funeral walk	latch	noon	quail	small bridge	whitefish
bougainvillea	dogwood	garfish	lavender	Northeasterly	quince	smallfry	whitewash
boulder	dolphin	geranium	lemon tree	North wind	radishes	source	wild cherry
braided rug	donkey	ghost	licorice	oars	rascal	Sou'westerly	wild dove
bride	doublemint	girl	lighthearted	ochre	ravine	sparrow	wild goat
brine	dovecot	glare	lighthouse	octopus	red earth	spinning wheel	wild pear
butterfly	dragnet	goat	light-shadowed	offering	red lead	sprite	wind
café	dry	gooseberry	lily of the shore	oil lamp	red mullet	squall	windmill
cage	drystone	grandma	limpet	oil press	resin	stalactite	woodbine
caïque	dumb	grape	little bell	old man	rope	starfish	woven
canary	East wind	grass	little stairs	olive	rose	starlight	yard
candle	easy	gull	lizard	omelet	rosebush	stern	zephyr
candlestick	echo	gust	lobster	orange	rosemary	stone ship	zucchini
cape	eggplant	halter	locust	oregano	rowlock	stone sill	
captain	Eléni	hare	loom	Orion	ruins	storm	
cardamom	embers	harpoon	low wall	ouzo	saddle	strait	

ODYSSEAS ELYTIS (Translated by Olga Broumas)

The history of the house in this book is not one of stagnation; a house and a garden need

constant nurturing. Towels go gray or fray, cushions tear, carpets fade, plants die and must

be replaced, trees grow too close together and need to be cut down — it is not dreary

maintenance that is necessary but the celebration of life itself.

A house, your living space, is a sanctuary. Your bed is where you dream. Your kitchen is where you drink coffee or juice, eat breakfast, perhaps lunch and dinner too. Whether it is a room, a house, an apartment, or a loft in Paris, New York, Rio, or Mumbai, your sanctuary reflects your personality.

A house lived in for decades by the same person, or indeed centuries by the same family, emanates an atmosphere of old loves, lost friends, past thoughts, agreements and disagreements, happiness and misery. It is a palpable and telling atmosphere that can be sinister and threatening, joyous and soothing. A happy family will have a happy house, regardless of taste and decoration. Sophistication and style are not analogous to happiness, which springs rather from comfort, good manners, colors that please the eye, works of art, flowers, and cherished objects. A vista from room to room, onto a terrace or garden, a view of Manhattan glittering at night or Rome at dusk, the sound of a train passing, a dog barking or laughter in the street, water lapping against the stones of Venice, the smell of freshly mown grass through an open window — these are gifts that enhance the world you have created. Discriminating or not, the choices you make will always reflect your habits, thoughts, and inclinations.

14

PART ONE

THE ISLAND

BY SUSANNA MOORE

I John, who also am yout brother, and companion, and in the kingdom and

patience of Jesus Christ, was in the isle that is called Patmos…

REVELATION OF ST. JOHN THE DIVINE [REV 1:9]

THE PEOPLE OF THE MEDITERRANEAN, as the name suggests, believed themselves to be at the very center of the world. The sea, connecting the three continents of Europe, Asia, and Africa, extends from Gibraltar to the Bosphorus; from Spain, France, and Italy, sliding past the old seaports of Barcelona, Genoa, and Venice to Croatia, Albania, Greece, and Turkey. It passes, among others, the cities of Tunis, Zagreb, and Benghazi, encircling the islands of Sardinia, Corsica, Sicily, Crete, the Cyclades, the Dodecanese, and Cyprus, to reach the far coasts of Syria, Lebanon, Israel, Egypt, Libya, Tunisia, Algeria, and Morocco.

The Eastern Mediterranean — known as the Levant — has been inhabited by humans for 100,000 years, its people steadily spreading across the sea as some civilizations flourished, and others declined, or disappeared. Although the diversity of languages, customs, systems of writing, political economies, and religions is exceedingly wide, Mediterranean peoples are joined by their proximity to and affinity for the sea. The unusual energy of movement — whether of slaves captured in war or pirate raids, pilgrims undertaking the perilous journey to the Holy Land, soldiers sailing south to Tangier or Cairo, or traders and adventurers darting recklessly past the Straits of Gibraltar in search of lucrative routes to the East — has

19

LOOKING DOWN on the port of Skala with Ikaria and Samos in the distance.

given to its people a sophistication, tolerance, and versatility not common to the inhabitants of more restricted (and colder) regions.

This fluid world, made vivid in the work of Homer and Herodotus, has been subject for thousands of years to invasion and emigration. This admixture of cultures is readily apparent in the influence of the Muslim world on the architecture and music of Spain; the churches of Italy, decorated with Byzantine mosaics; the temple of Syracuse, one of the cities of Magna Graecia in Sicily; and in the great library of Alexandria, which contained the plays, many of them now lost, of Aeschylus and Euripides. The Latin genius is as resplendent in the Baroque temples at Baalbek, as is the Moorish apprehension of shade and light evident in the arched windows of a Venetian palace. The farmhouses of Provence, the capacious tents of the Bedouin, the stone mountain forts built by the Crusaders in Lebanon, and the terra-cotta brick towers of the Libyan desert are singularly idiosyncratic and singularly indigenous. The food of the Mediterranean in itself constitutes a long history of disparate, even antithetical cultures — foods to which we are now accustomed, but which were once distant, strange, and mystifying to us: pine nuts, avocados, dates, pomegranates, tarragon and basil, peppers, eggplant, red mullet, octopus, and stingrays.

VIEW OF SKALA and the harbor from Chora.

The twelve islands known in Greek as the Dodecanese lie north of Crete and the Cyclades to run along the coast of Asia Minor. The volcanic island of Patmos, one of the smallest islands in the Aegean, is twenty-one square miles, with a coastline of forty miles. There are eleven large bays on the island, and numerous small, uninhabited islands along the coast. An outpost of the geology of southern Turkey, Patmos sits on the eastern rim of a volcanic basin. The sea is nearly eleven thousand feet deep in places — only the greatest of its mountains break the surface.

The island consists of two landmasses, joined by a slender strip of sand several hundred yards wide. It has a population of approximately three thousand people, although the number climbs to twenty thousand with the flood of visitors who arrive in the month of August. The main settlements are Skala, Kampos, Chora, and Grikou. Thanks to its safe harborage, Skala

(the name means both stairway and landing place) was once the refuge of pirates, whose raids accounted for the frequent abandonment of the island. Chora, as well as the monastery of St. John the Divine and the Cave of the Apocalypse, were designated World Heritage Sites by UNESCO in 1999.

The climate of the Mediterranean is generally mild, with wet winters and hot summers. The coastline tends to be arid. In the woods, there are oak and pine. Wheat is the dominant crop, as well as lemons, figs, and grapes, although some historians simply define the Mediterranean as the place where olive trees grow. The island, dry most of the year, the colors of its ravines and hills a rust-brown thanks to its foundation of igneous rock, is transformed in spring by the cistus, broom, and euphorbia that cover the hills, dotted here and there by wild crocuses and asphodels. Due to the lack of good soil and rainfall, there is not an abundance of cultivated land. Small land holdings are separated by low walls of gray stone topped with layers of furze to discourage wandering goats. The island is without rivers, and there is only a handful of small springs. There is the occasional cypress and palm tree. The Patmians grow oranges, lemons, pomegranates, prickly pear, and figs. There are snakes on the island — a long and slender snake that moves like a dart is called the Arrow-Snake — and numerous seabirds and partridges. Sheep and goats are kept, as well as donkeys for labor (there are few horses or cows), and the flocks, in the long, nostalgic monotony of antiquity, graze across the arid hills. There are not many roads, even today, and footpaths lie in the beds of dry brooks, the old tracks running downhill to the coast, as they have for thousands of years. There is no lushness, and the pleasing austerity of the landscape is reflected in the island's architecture. It is under the surface of the sea that life flourishes: fish and shellfish, porpoise and coral, squid and algae, sea grass and kelp.

22

THE *MAQUIS* in early summer: *Verbascum bombiferum, Genista acanthoclada, Euphorbia acanthothamnos, Sarcopoterium spinosum.*

OVERLEAF:
Gathering wheat.

By good fortune, it is the Virgin Deer-Hunter herself that appointed the renowned daughter of Glaukias the physician her own priestess; to bear water, and sacrifice by the altar … the birthplace of the family … that brought her up is Patmos, the most illustrious island of Artemis, the daughter of Leto, whose protector she became, saving its foundations in the depths of the sea, since the time when the warlike Orestes brought and installed her from Scythia after she had saved him from the terrible madness after the murder of his mother.

—Inscription found in excavations on Castelli

Patmos is said to have been named in honor of the sea god, Poseidon, who once honored the island with a visit. Other historians believe that Orestes took refuge on Patmos in his flight from the Furies after the murder of his mother, Clytemnestra. It is generally accepted, however, that Patmos is the illustrious island of Artemis, twin sister of Apollo and goddess of the moon, chastity, wild beasts, and the hunt. Temples to Artemis were found throughout the Mediterranean in the ancient world; what remains to us are the famous refuge of Diana in Ephesus, and Cyrene in Libya, as well as sanctuaries to the goddess in Delos, Aphrodisias, Knidos, Marseilles, Syracuse, Pamphylia, and Miletus.

As is befitting an island of the goddess Artemis, Patmos is redolent with myth, superstition, and spirits. The temple of Artemis is said to have been built on the acropolis overlooking the port of Skala. An enclosure that may once have held a statue of the bee goddess is still visible among the rocks and crevices of the citadel of Castelli, high above the harbor. The fortification walls, once seven feet thick and made of dark local stone, are dated to the fourth century BC. The temple remained in use as late as 1088 AD, when the Christian abbot Christodopolus flung a statue of Artemis into the sea, putting an end to her long and glorious reign. Patmos, like other outposts of the ancient world, was to receive over centuries the benefit of a Christian flowering, which, despite its enormous influence and continuing power, did not altogether succeed in eliminating the lingering ghosts of the old gods who lived on to haunt the ruins of their sanctuaries.

Nicholas Poussin, *Landscape
with St. John on Patmos,* 1640.
Photography © Art Institute
of Chicago.

OVERLEAF:
Farming the land.

In the fifth century AD, the historian Thucydides mentioned the island — much of
ancient Greek history took place in the nearby cities of Asia Minor — but by the seventh
century, thanks to marauding pirates, the island was uninhabited. Pliny the Elder wrote that
desolate Patmos was a place of frequent banishment, particularly from Ephesus, sixty miles
across the sea to the northeast, where the evangelist St. John is said to have taken refuge
after the Crucifixion with Mary, the mother of Jesus.

There are numerous legends and folktales surrounding the arrival of St. John on Patmos
in 925 AD. It is not certain that he was banished to Patmos, or if he took refuge there; it is
possible that he fled precipitously to the obscure island to live safely until the persecutions

THE ISLAND

ordered by Rome had lessened. Despite the conflicting views of academics and historians, it is common knowledge on the island that after a number of trials, the saint defeated the wicked magician Kynops, who lived in a cave near the harbor of Grikou. John, in the company of his familiar, an eagle, is said to have worked many miracles, including the restoring to life of three children, as well as rescuing the child of the sea captain whose ship carried John to Patmos. Having successfully converted the Patmians during the ten years of his stay, St. John prepared to return to Ephesus, but the Christians pleaded with him not to abandon them. When they could not persuade him, they asked that he put the mystery of Christ into writing. He retired to a cave on a low hill behind the port of Skala, where he remained for three days, fasting and praying in hope that the Holy Spirit would descend upon him to give him the Word of God. At last, a flash of lightning and thunder shook the hillside. John looked to the heavens and instructed his acolyte, Prochoros, to begin writing: "In the beginning was the Word."

Some modern scholars contend that St. John was witness to a particularly violent volcanic eruption on the island of Thera, which he described as a "beast rising out of the sea" (REV. 13:1), or that he saw a phenomenon of lightning common to the skies over nearby Samos. The Revelation — that mysterious, strange, transcendental hallucination — is so full of images reminiscent of Patmos that it is impossible not to conclude that John, like others before and after him, had fallen under the spell of the island's singular beauty: "the sky vanished like a scroll that is rolled up, and every mountain and island was removed from its place" (REV. 6:14). "Every island fled away, and no mountains were to be found; and great hailstones, heavy as a hundred-weight, dropped on men from heavens" (REV. 16:20–21).

DUE TO ITS ARIDITY AND ISOLATION, and weakened by the raids of marauding pirates, the island fell into dereliction, remaining abandoned for nearly two hundred years until the arrival in 1088 of the Abbot of Latros, Christodopolous, with his ambitions to build a great monastery in honor of St. John. He carried with him a title deed from Alexios Comnenos, Byzantine emperor in Constantinople, to secure the islands of the Aegean against the marauding Turks, and granting the abbot the right to Patmos ("My one desire," wrote Christodopolous, "was to possess this island"), as well as to farms on Samos and Crete. Christodopolous had chosen Patmos as the site of his monastery because it was sparsely inhabited, possessed a fine harbor and, not least, because the island's inhospitality made it particularly conducive to intellectual and aesthetic pursuits — in truth, there was little for a holy man to do on the island. A fellow monk wrote, "I did not want to go there … because Patmos was far away, the trip to reach the island was full of hardships, the danger from the Turkish warships and the pirates was great, and also because the island itself was deserted and difficult to tread."

The foundations for the monastery were laid soon after Christodopolous's arrival, and great stone walls were raised to protect the site from Arab raids. A four-column, cross-in-square domed church was built; the Chapel of the Virgin and the Chapel of St. Christodopolous were later additions. A refectory was part of the original complex, as was a kitchen and six cells, and various outbuildings. A library was made to house the books that Christodopolous had brought with him from Asia Minor.

The monastery was to be organized as an idiorrhythmic retreat, meaning that each monk was permitted to retain his own property, to eat his meals alone in his cell if he so desired, and to determine the extent of his own religious and ascetic disciplines — practices that continue to this day. The Emperor Comnenos had wisely suggested that Christodopolus allow a small number of laymen to accompany the abbot to the island to lessen the trials of monastic life. The workmen, many of them refugees from Crete, soon rebelled without their womenfolk. There were outbreaks of typhus and malaria, and Christodopolous allowed the men to send for their families.

Christodopolous wrote in his autobiography that he instructed the monks "to work, each according to his talent" and to preserve the books in the library "most diligently." True to the wishes of its founder, the collection of Christodopolous was protected and, over the centuries, more treasures and books were acquired, so that today the monastery contains

ST. JOHN the Evangelist and Prochoros. Revelation Gospels Codex 81, Jul 238.

OVERLEAF:
A monk walking toward Chora.

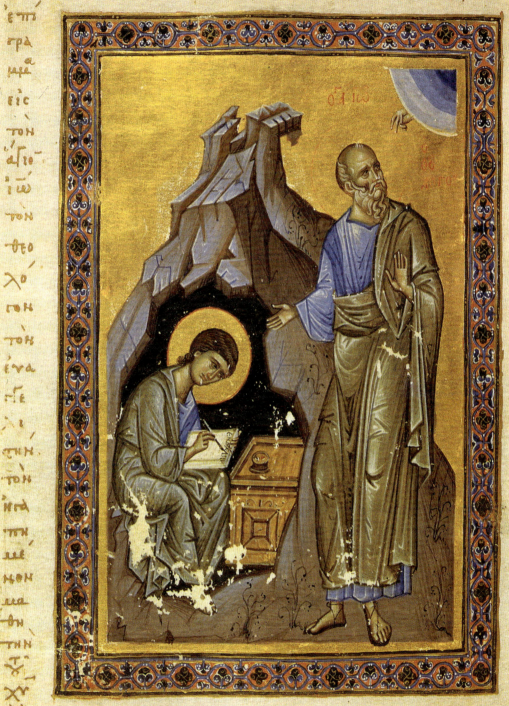

one thousand manuscripts, rare editions from the fifteenth and sixteenth centuries, a number

MONKS in Chora.

of Byzantine documents, and thirteen thousand modern Greek texts.

With the fall of Constantinople to the Turks in 1453, the island's population was increased with the arrival of refugees, who brought with them their more sophisticated ways. In 1454, with the expansion of the Ottoman empire, the Turks took possession of the island. The islands of the eastern Aegean did not suffer greatly under Ottoman rule, and the monastery was allowed to retain its privileges to keep a fleet of forty ships for trading throughout the Mediterranean. In the mid-seventeenth century, the island suffered during the wars fought

THE MONASTERY on the north side of Chora, photographed from the air.

THE COURTYARD of the
monastery of St. John.

ABOVE LEFT:
Ramparts of the monastery
of St. John.

ABOVE RIGHT:
An early Romanesque-style
window in the monastery with
carved Orthodox crosses on
either side.

between the Venetians and the Ottoman Turks for hegemony in the region. Venice had begun

to play a significant role in the Aegean in the eleventh century, often to the disadvantage of

Constantinople, and by the early thirteenth century the fortunes of the island shifted once

again. Thanks to the Venetians, Patmos became semiautonomous, gaining even greater wealth

and influence, despite the rapacious incursions of the Venetian fleet. In 1659 an anonymous

Patmian diarist wrote: "The entire fleet of the Venetians arrived, over eight hundred ships,

and they came ashore. We estimated that they carried off almost half a million in silver, gold,

and other riches."

At the end of the Turkish-Venetian wars in 1669, fortifications had been built as a precaution against the raids from North Africa. Patmos has always been dependent on the outside world for prosperity — now as well as then — and the island relied heavily on trading ships and the commerce and wayfarers they carried, as well as warships in search of a good harbor. The Patmians, seamen in the service of the monastery, had become accomplished shipbuilders, navigators, and merchants, sailing to France, Russia, Egypt, and England to trade pottery and

A SAIL on the horizon and Patmos beyond.

cotton stockings knitted by the women. With their growing wealth, the traders gained equal rights with the monks in regard to property and the economy of the island, building grand houses in Chora, which they filled with the bounty of their travels: furniture, icons, silver, china, and textiles. This period of prosperity lasted until the end of sail; with the use of steamships, the venturesome Patmians transferred their attention abroad, and their opulent mansions were deserted. The age of emigration had begun — the men joined the merchant marine or left for Russia and Egypt (and more recently Texas and Australia).

THE RUINS OF THE TEMPLE OF ARTEMIS on the acropolis of Castelli were not discovered until 1817, when two marble fragments were found, one of them a sepulchral tablet of a dog waiting at the side of his dying master. In 1850 the traveler M. Guérin described an old monk named Apollou, who had made for himself a small refuge on the northeastern coast called Thermia, now known as the Hermitage (where visitors may nap in the shade of the monk's grape arbor). Apollou planted a small orchard and used the neighboring spring to grow vegetables and vines. "At nine o'clock, he conducted me to my cell and then retired to his own," wrote Guérin. "Toward midnight I heard him rise with the other three monks, and soon I heard their voices united in the chapel; his voice sounded above them all, and gave the chant a sweet harmony. I was very much moved in the silence of the night when, at the foot of a solitary mountain, and only a few steps from the sea, whose murmur, an eternal complaint, reached my ears, I heard suddenly four voices, which chanted a prayer in a chorus that animated this desert region."

By the nineteenth century, the people of the island were once again diminished in number, as the vigorous trade between islands and countries disappeared. The hillsides had long been decimated of timber, and charcoal, burned in low metal braziers, was used in the damp winters to warm the drafty houses. There was seldom meat to eat, and the land was difficult to cultivate. In 1912 the Italians took possession of the island during a war with Turkey and remained on Patmos through World War II, when the island was at last returned by Italy to Greece.

41

OVERLEAF:
The M/S boat *Poseidon*. The valiant Captain Vassilis at the helm of this seaworthy vessel carries me and my guests across azure waters. Sea urchins, a local delicacy, are eaten raw, plucked fresh from the sea. My two Boston terriers, Sugar and Pinky, are intrepid voyagers.

PART TWO

THE HOUSE

BY SUSANNA MOORE

Somewhere among the notebooks of Gideon, I once found a list of diseases as yet unclassified by medical science, and among these occurred the word *Islomania*, which was described as a rare but by no means unknown affliction of spirit. There are people, Gideon used to say, by way of explanation, who find islands somehow irresistible. The mere knowledge that they are on an island, a little world surrounded by the sea, fills them with an indescribable intoxication. These born "islomanes," he used to add, are the direct descents of the Atlanteans, and it is towards the lost Atlantis that their subconscious yearns throughout their island life…

LAWRENCE DURRELL, *Reflections on a Marine Venus*

THE HOUSE with its garden, the small chapel of St. George and St. Eustace, and olive groves. Behind the house is the church of St. Mary the Saviour. The town of Chora spreads itself around the fortified walls of the majestic monastery of St. John.

SO IT WAS THAT ONE HOT SUMMER in 1963, two curious Atlanteans, John Stefanidis and the late Teddy Millington-Drake, landed at the harbor of Skala on the island of Patmos. The young men had been sailing in the eastern Mediterranean, stopping at every small island as they slowly traveled north. The journey from Rhodes to Patmos had taken eighteen hours in an old boat laden with animals.

They arrived at noon, a haunted hour (Theocritus warned against too much fervor in the midday hour: "not at noon, we may not pipe at noon, for Pan we dread, who then comes from the chase weary and takes his rest"). The northwest Etesian wind, called the *meltemi*, did little to appease the summer heat. Small steamers lay at anchor in the port, as well as the shallow hulled wooden caiques used by fishermen, but the island was not prosperous. In the harbor, several carved, white marble columns, once used in the portico of the temple of Artemis, served as mooring posts.

In need of lodging and food, the two men climbed the hill behind the harbor to the medieval town of Chora, built against the ramparts of the monastery of St. John. On the hillside behind Skala, there was a cattle pen made of marble, taken from the sanctuary of Artemis (there is said to have been a hippodrome on the island, but its location has never been found). The road led past the Patmiada School for religious training and the dark grotto where St. John wrote the Apocalypse, climbing gently to the row of elegant hillside mansions built in the nineteenth century for the rich merchants and shipbuilders of the town. The writer and traveler Lawrence Durrell, who visited Patmos during World War II, described the climb to Chora: "We entered ... and found ourselves immediately in a warren of cobbled streets, each just wide enough for the passage of a loaded mule, and thrown down upon each other in a sort of labyrinth ... up stairways, down alleys, round corners, doubling back upon ourselves at different levels until we found the great door of the monastery.... From every nook now the prospect began to shine out, the brilliant bay and the further seas, set in green and grey."

The walk had changed little in the twenty years since Durrell had stopped there (later, Millington-Drake and Stefanidis had the benefit of taking the one taxi on the island, commandeered by a gentleman named Georgio, famous for his imitations of birdsong). At the top of the hill, they found a small paved square, the Platia Loza (also known as Xanthos), surrounded by large, nineteenth-century houses that overlooked the sea and the shadowed islands beyond. To this day, no cars are allowed in the town of Chora — the flagged lanes are too narrow and winding.

During Easter week, when small dolls like Cycladic goddesses, known as *lazarakia*, are baked in bread, the square and streets are strewn with wild lavender. It is possible, on a fine day, to see the distant coast of Asia forty miles across the sea, and the islands of Ikaria, Fourni,

SMALL BREAD DOLLS, reminiscent of Cycladic scuplture, have been baked at Easter for centuries.

THE LABYRINTHINE streets of Chora climb their way to the monastery.

16

and Samos afloat on the wine-dark sea. The traveler William Geil wrote, "It is easy to think of the exile (St. John) climbing to gaze wistfully across and pray for the persecuted. The Aegean has a beauty of its own, not the dark blue of the Mediterranean, nor the marine green of the deep Atlantic, but it may have glistened in the seer's eyes under the rising sun like a 'sea of glass mingled with fire.'"

The beauty of Chora is of a meticulous Aegean order. The winding lanes, here and there paved with sea pebbles, are laced with alleys, and the vaulted passageways, roofed with cane, are just wide enough for two mules abreast. The high, flat walls of the houses conceal the small gardens and courtyards within — it is only the sudden scent of a fig tree or a spill of plumbago that reveals the secrets hidden behind the thick walls.

Chora was still close to abandoned when Millington-Drake and Stefanidis landed on the island. Many of the houses, derelict behind crumbling yellow stucco walls (the walls had not been whitewashed in generations), were empty. There were two dusty cafes and one food shop. Occasionally, they had a glimpse through an open door to a courtyard where basil and jasmine grew in rusty tin cans. The inhabitants of the little town were kind and generous, demonstrating their customary island hospitality with prompt offers of coffee accompanied by a spoonful of homemade citrus jam, or a fresh gardenia. (As far as the men could make out, there were, in the middle of August, only two other foreigners on the island.) Some of the older residents spoke Italian, learned during the thirty-five years of occupation by the Italian army. A local man, Mr. Kapranis, and his wife were helpful to the strangers; fortunately, they spoke English, having owned a tobacco shop on Shaftesbury Avenue in London for twenty years. The mayor, Mr. Valas, took the two men around the island in his little boat, dropping them for the day at one of the many isolated bays or islets, and collecting them again at sunset.

Stefanidis remembers that Chora possessed the beauty of a de Chirico painting. "There were sweeps of olive groves, titan rocks plunging into the sea, bays of pristine beauty with gently lapping waves … and everywhere the sea: aquamarine, turquoise, emerald green, deep purple. The old myths and symbols were everywhere — the pull of the Orthodox remains strong alongside Asia Minor."

With no thought of resistance, the two travelers did not take long to succumb (a friend,

TOP LEFT:
The Town Hall.
TOP RIGHT:
A passageway with a pointed arch.
BELOW LEFT:
Rounded arches lined with wooden beams and branches bleached white over centuries.
BELOW RIGHT:
Steps (of which there are hundreds) wind their way from house to house.

AN AXONOMETRIC drawing of
the house done by students from
an architectural school in Salonika.

the writer Bruce Chatwin, who later came to Patmos to write and windsurf, said that the island was no place for emotional weaklings). By the end of that first summer, Millington-Drake and Stefanidis began negotiations to buy a sixteenth-century farmhouse in Chora. The house, stretching across the side of a hill, sat peacefully at the edge of a small, silent square (where, twenty years later, one of the two pay telephones on the island would appear). On three levels, the property descended through terraced gardens to fields enclosed by neglected stone walls. There was an Old Testament view across the dry fields to the eighteenth-century hermitage of the Prophet Elijah, sitting serenely atop the highest hill on the island.

The house, abandoned for twenty-five years, was bought from the Diakoyanni family for one thousand pounds. It had sound thick walls, old carved doors, and bleached wood floors. The house comprised the rooms that end with Stefanidis's bedroom on the first floor and the guest bathroom and bedroom on the second floor. At the bottom of the derelict terrace garden was a double-vaulted, whitewashed private chapel dedicated to St. George and St. Eustace. Stefanidis had the strong sense that the house had been loved. Records show that in 1636, it had belonged to a Russian merchant named Syfantos. His daughter married a man from Crete, and their daughter married a man from Kos, ensuring that the house was passed from daughter to daughter, as is the Greek tradition, for generations.

Stefanidis returned to Patmos that winter, persuading a plumber and an electrician to travel from the Greek mainland to the remote island. There were oil lamps in the house for light, and rainwater was collected in cisterns. Parts of the house had collapsed. The walls, previously altered to make a terrace for farming, had been constructed with such style and simplicity that only after careful scrutiny was it apparent that some of the terraces had not always been there. A simple bathroom was made with a pump that sent water to a tank on the roof. The men patched and whitewashed the walls, and a window was opened in a storeroom, but the house was not altered structurally.

The one good builder on the island, Tomas Ypsilantis, a dashing man with a white moustache and a black dog, began work on the restoration of the house (over the years, he and Stefanidis would restore more than ten houses together). One of the local stonemasons improvised a rough sketch of a sea monster to decorate the floor of a terrace, using small

A SEA MONSTER made of pebbles carried from a local beach naps on the Lemon Terrace.

stones carried up from the beach. The Patmians, Stefanidis realized, possessed a natural sense of the use of stone and brick, a dying skill that, thanks to Stefanidis, was soon revived. He coaxed local carpenters into remaking the doors and windows in the seldom-used but traditional way — a style that has since become common throughout the island. Tables and chairs were designed, and cupboards and armoires were made with panels of wood latticework. An old style of backless sofa, once inspired by a rich merchant's Empire settee, was made by a local carpenter named Vassous Nikitakis. Much of the furniture and the molding and trim of the interiors were painted cerulean blue, reminiscent of the sky. In keeping with the vernacular of the island — architecture without architects — whitewashed walls, tiled floors, scrubbed boards, local pottery, and embroidery were part of a deliberate strategy to maintain the fantasy of the past in a world of comfort.

In 1964, a year after climbing onto the quay in Skala, Stefanidis and Millington-Drake

AN EMBROIDERY typical of the Dodecanese Islands in a geometric design of stylized flowers and foliage. From their mothers and grandmothers, girls learned traditional techniques of needlework, often particular to their island, using linen, cotton, or silk, and vegetable dyes made on the island. These embroideries were an important part of a girl's trousseau.

spent their first summer in the house. In March, with the fresh spring winds, swallows had built their nests in the eaves of the house, and wild orchids were in bloom beneath the lemon trees. The cistus made a cloud of pink across the valley. Millington-Drake and Stefanidis wanted to keep the spell of the sacred island intact for as long as possible. Stefanidis smilingly remembers that when the occasional tourist happened on Patmos by chance, his impulse was to close the shutters and refuse to answer a knock on the door.

At the end of the summer, Stefanidis returned to Italy to find himself longing for the Aegean. "After the clarity of Greece (a brush with the gods that confirmed my paganism), Milan was untenable," he wrote. He moved to Athens, a city that was "old-fashioned still, with a sparkling sky streaming at night with shooting stars and, in those days, the cleanest air in Europe.... The Greek temperament, more tempestuous and pleasure-loving than that of northern Italy, suited me. I embarked on my own ... odyssey."

A VIEW from the upper terrace toward Grikou, now mostly hidden by tall cypress trees.

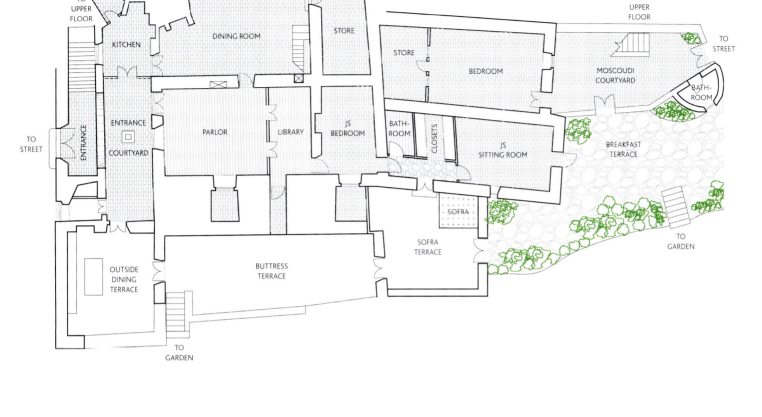

LABYRINTHIAN FIRST FLOOR

(in which many guests have lost their way)

THERE IS A COURTYARD (which is the main entrance of the house) and off it a kitchen; stone steps leading to the top floor; a door leading to the outside dining room (there is also an inside dining room); a parlor leading to a library, my bedroom, bathroom, and sitting room, and, through a door, the breakfast terrace. A step up is the Moscoudi courtyard, which has a hidden door leading to the maze of streets, and off it a guest bedroom and bathroom and stone steps that lead to the terrace above — a labyrinth indeed.

OVERLEAF:
A view of the house in the early 1980s, with the newly paved and planted Lemon Terrace.

PERHAPS BECAUSE JOHN STEFANIDIS was born on the coast of Egypt in the ancient port city of Alexandria, he understands intuitively what it means to belong to the Mediterranean. He possesses an acute sensitivity to light and shade: nowhere does the crushing weight of the noonday sun invade his peaceful house or garden, nor does the vertiginous introspection of shadow render one melancholic. His memory, full of history, enables him to connect the past to the present. His sense of style concerns itself with layers of the past, tempered by a sensibility that is modern. It is the way of islands, where the days are long and full of changing light, and nothing is held too fiercely. There is nothing precious or sentimental. Islands, like the past, are not made to bear nostalgia.

"What might be called Mediterranean style," says Stefanidis, "is in many ways a conceit, given the numerous layers of civilizations, cultures, and influences that contribute to it; a conceit that is composed of romanticism, sensuality, and practicality. Mediterranean style is a triumph of common sense. Whitewashed walls reflect light and heat; thick walls render rooms cool; cotton furnishings are fresher to the touch and the eye than wool and velvet. Lattice allows air to circulate; shutters exclude glare; tile and marble are soothing to the bare foot." A bench or day bed, where one can draw up one's legs and sit cross-legged, is not as enveloping as a deep-cushioned sofa, and a bed draped in muslin filters the morning sun without stifling the breeze or shutting out the light. "The most valuable gift of the Mediterranean to domestic life is the seamlessness between inside and outside: there is no psychic separation between the two, thanks to rooms that open to terraces, terraces that spill into vegetation, gardens that stretch to open land. The secrets of the garden and the wilderness beyond are lured inside, and your world is composed of the colors of sky and sea — the startling blue of midday, the coral of sunset, the pale gray of dawn. The open rooms are full of the scent of the earth, and the smell of the not-too-distant sea."

Each door on the first floor of the house opens to a long terrace draped in jasmine and bougainvillea, flanked on one side by a row of buttresses, meant to support the house in an earthquake, and on the other side by the large garden descending the hillside in planted terraces — the old terra-cotta oil jars brimming with hibiscus and bougainvillea struggle to hold at bay the dense garden. There is a small terrace outside the carved door of Stefanidis's

58

A DOORWAY to the street from the Moscoudi courtyard covered by a blue and white canvas curtain crowned by a scrambling branch of *Bougainvillea glabra 'Sanderiana.'* A sunflower stands proudly in a terra-cotta pot above the gray rosettes of the succulent *Echeveria secunda.*

sitting room, where a traditional Greek breakfast is served each morning and China tea in the afternoon, among banks of basil, roses, and jasmine.

I T HAS BEEN SAID that the work of John Stefanidis, no matter the location, shimmers with the light of the islands. That the objects and furniture he chooses for rooms possess a proper and unerring weight, place, and substance. The grandest items are used in an easy and spontaneous way: an antique Turkish textile in a stone bathroom; a seventeenth-century Damascus chest illuminated by brass lanterns from the Istanbul souk. With a sensitivity to light, shade, and color, as well as the knowledge that accompanies and even necessitates the long view, Stefanidis conveys meaning with little, finding the subtle balance between pattern and freedom, wit and simplicity, tradition and the play of fancy. It is a style composed of the rich, heavily laden historical past, translated into a deceptively simple domestic luxury that encompasses and celebrates light and shade, sky and sea. In 1968 the writer and archaeologist Freya Stark wrote in a thank-you note after a month's stay in the house, "It is a work of art you have inserted in the unexpected, bright frame of the islands."

The main entrance of the house, which once faced the street at the foot of the large church of St. Mary the Saviour, had been moved to a narrow side alley in 1850 (it is said that a secret passage once ran from the kitchen of the house to the church). A visitor steps through a heavy wooden door from bright sunlight into the cool respite of a large interior courtyard. There is a view to the terrace beyond, where a stone dining table and bench sit in a haze of plumbago and white oleander. An exterior staircase, shaded by an old grapevine, climbs past the kitchen to a second-floor terrace.

One moves from the solace of the courtyard into the downstairs visitor's parlor, where blue and white Chinese porcelain, mixed with Spode plates in a spinach pattern and old Flora Danica once used by Millington-Drake's grandmother, sits peacefully in a glass cabinet. Behind the parlor, there is a large dining room with the oldest beams in the house, the wood blackened with smoke from the bread oven, and a tiled floor bearing the hoof marks of the donkeys who once lived there. Behind the parlor there is a small library, as well as Stefanidis's bedroom, bathroom, and sitting room. Climbing the stairs to the second floor, the visitor enters the

60

A SEVENTEENTH-CENTURY chest from Damascus, inlaid with typical mother-of-pearl motifs found all over the Mediterranean. On top is a Persian mirror on a stand with a sun motif in gilt, possibly Zoroastrian. On either side are JS-designed large storm lanterns. Handmade Patmiote tiles are on the floor.

long, cool room known as the White Room, alongside a large sitting room with a triptych by Millington-Drake and a vast Patmian sofa. There is a small Turkish room with red-and-white-striped mattresses and appliquéd cushions in Oriental designs, and a bedroom, just large enough for a nineteenth-century iron four-poster bed that was found on the island.

62

LEFT:
Whitewashed stone steps
outside the kitchen window
lead from the entrance
courtyard to the upper
terrace.

RIGHT:
The courtyard is built over a
vast cistern. Hats on the wall
fit all tastes and sizes. A large
terra-cotta amphora stands
guard beneath a Venetian tin
lantern, held aloft by a gilded
wooden lion's paw jutting
from the wall. The beams are
unpainted wood and the
boards in between are
painted pale pink.

LEFT:

A view of the kitchen and staircase. The grapevine was planted when the house was bought in the 1960s; its flowers and fruit now spill onto the upper terrace.

BELOW AND RIGHT:

A wooden rail laden with scarves for guests on a cool evening. A traditional English fish basket with Japanese umbrellas, some made of cloth, others of paper.

ABOVE AND RIGHT:

Tin lanterns surround a Boston fern in a large basket sold by gypsies who travel from island to island selling their wares.

Wooden trays from Turkish markets are in constant use. Once piled with fresh fish and vegetables, they have been painted in different colors.

OUTSIDE DINING TERRACE

A book with a drawing by Teddy Millington-Drake
of the view toward the outdoor dining terrace.
In the distance is the chapel of the Prophet Elijah,
once the site of a temple to Apollo.

OPPOSITE:

TOP LEFT: Although the plantings of
Nerium oleander have grown to hide
the chapel, they serve as an
effective wind break.

TOP RIGHT: A fragment of a carved
Ghandara frieze.

BOTTOM LEFT: A rustic chair in the
corner of the terrace. After thirty
years, all chairs and stools were
replaced. Made in mainland Greece
to a JS design, they are slightly
wider than traditional taverna chairs
and more comfortable.

BOTTOM RIGHT: Antique stone
fragments on a terrace wall.

LEFT:

On the dining terrace, a stone bench with white unadorned squabs. A JS Patmos tray holds blue spiraled Venetian glasses.

RIGHT:

A detail of the stone dining table. The white striped carafe for water is part of a set designed for the house and made in Venice by Laura de Santillana.

SECTIONS OF SOLID STONE from a local quarry
are supported by whitewashed columns.
The table is set without mats, a foil to the plates
designed by M-D of enameled porcelain. The
striped glasses are part of the set designed for the
house. The long-necked wine carafes are the
same as those depicted in seventeenth-century
Italian paintings. In the bowls are the zinnias that
flower all summer in shades of madder pink,
ochre, and alma brown.

THE KITCHEN

72

A VIEW THROUGH to the kitchen from the entrance courtyard. On the left is an Italian wooden chair with an armorial chest topped by a Cardinal's hat — a daring intrusion in a bastion of orthodoxy. The kitchen is painted Adonis blue, otherwise known as Bleu de France. The top shelf displays part of a set of pottery in an olive branch pattern once made by artisans on Crete.

74

FRESH VEGETABLES are kept in bowls on a raised platform in the kitchen to thwart the island's ubiquitous mice.

THE KITCHEN WINDOW — unaltered since the house was purchased. I would have designed it differently but I respect its quirkiness. On a tray are glasses, silver salt cellars and pepper pots, knives and forks ready for the dining table.

THE DINING ROOM

This room with its whitewashed arch has a long, built-in stone seat with cushions and a locally made trestle table and wooden bench. The mammoth beams with twigs and bamboo wedged between are blackened with age. Some of the terra-cotta floor tiles have been broken by the hooves of donkeys from the time when animals were housed on the ground floor. It is from this room that there may have been a passage leading to the church of St. Mary the Saviour.

THE LARGE CUSHIONS on the stone bench are in
cotton toile in a shade of terra-cotta known as
cremorne. The cushions are a mixture of a JS-printed
design, Patmiote and Anatolian needlework — some
embroidered and others woven on a *kilim* loom.

The table laid for dinner. Lemons in a silver-gilt basket
are flanked by Georgian candlesticks.

ABOVE
A plate rack with Millington-Drake
enameled ceramic plates.

RIGHT
The table in the corner is used for more
intimate dining. A *suzani* curtain can be
pulled across the door to the parlor. In
the foreground are plates from the
island of Skyros, a set of plates depicting
the *seasous* from Este in the Veneto, and
English brown and white plates once
owned by a Patmiote sea captain. The
stairs lead to the anteroom painted by
M-D.

THE PARLOR

The parlor has recently been brightened with the addition of a JS-designed *kilim* in an enlarged Anatolian pattern with a hyacinth blue background. The two JS Rothschild chairs are covered loosely in sky-blue cotton. The doors with glazed panels are an architectural motif found throughout the island. On the wall, an eighteenth-century Venetian gilt mirror (found in Chora) hangs above a Moghul inlaid ivory chest sent from India in the 1820s to be Japanned in England — examples of many migratory pieces that link the island to the rest of the world.

83

OVERLEAF:
On the right, an antique map of Venice next to a vitrine displaying Flora Danica plates. A rustic Baroque eighteenth-century Italian chair sits on the pale, time-bleached wooden floor.

A TRADITIONAL island sofa, with
mattress-type cushions covered
in a JS fabric and cushions of
Anatolian needlework. The plate
on the wall is seventeenth-century
Italian majolica. The low table is
Indian, inset with mother-of-pearl,
a theme throughout the house.
The blue table — picked out in red
— is a JS design used elsewhere in
the house although painted in
different colors.

THE TABLE holds silver Egyptian coffee pots, an articulated silver fish from Colombia, a Russian cigarette box, a Peruvian *maté* spoon. In a corner of the downstairs parlor, two large parchment maps face each other across the room, stretched by painted wooden poles at the top and bottom. A Millington-Drake watercolor of Chilomodi — an island of mystery and beauty — sits on a trestle beside a *repoussé* Indian bowl brimful with pale blue *Senecio cineraria* freshly picked from the garden. The brass inlay chest, once used on dhows to transport spices and textiles, is from Zanzibar. On the right, a sofa with cushions made from Patmiote, Rhodian, and Turkish embroideries is of an earlier design than the Empire-style sofas seen in other rooms. The standing lamp has a tin shade, useful in its longevity.

IN THE PARLOR is an eighteenth-century mirror and an Indian ivory box atop a Moghul chest. The windows above the doors are a typical architectural detail on Patmos and were added to ensure more light — the M-D watercolor shows the room before the addition of the fanlights. There is a view through the carved wooden doors to the library.

THE LIBRARY

The small library at the heart of the first floor is full of books. The downstairs parlor is visible, and beyond that the entrance courtyard. Bookshelves on either side of a door or indeed above doors are always a successful device. The *dhurries*, cotton rugs from India, in Etruscan red and pistachio green stripes edged in black, were woven for the room. Below, a Turkish door curtain — silk with black stripes and silver embroidery at the hem — leads to my bedroom.

THE WALL-TO-WALL sofa has needlework cushions from Patmos, Rhodes, and Anatolia. The central cushion with a large tulip design is contemporary embroidery from an Athens workshop. Everything else in the room is Indian — the plaster figures on a shelf dressed in fabric clothes, the M-D drawings and watercolors of temples in South India, the golden *passementerie* mirrors. The miniatures are of Indian gods, or different castes in costumes particular to their trade or occupation. The table in the center was painted in a naïve manner by a Patmiote boatman, and more of his tables and stools are used throughout the house.

A view from the outdoor dining terrace to the buttress terrace.
Teddy Millington-Drake's painting shows that the doors were once
held open by stones, later replaced by carved and gilded white marble
door stops from Rajasthan. For thirty years, white pelargoniums have
been planted in pots by the corner of the stone bench. The blue and
white striped cushions are framed by bougainvillea, pruned into
exuberant balls of flame red and Udaipur pink.

THE BUTTRESS TERRACE
is shaded by an almond tree
(*Prunus dulcis*). A painted Turkish
tray on a stool holds a carafe of
wine, pistachios and chickpeas in
baskets, and a lemon for cocktails,
alongside a pile of monogrammed
paper napkins.

100 THE BLUE AND WHITE mattress
cushions are for resting or reading, and
for sitting with friends in the evening.
The small, low stools — typical of
Greece and central Asia — are
surprisingly comfortable. The stone
mortars are used to dispose of pistachio
shells or as an ashtray for a lone smoker.

THE SOFRA TERRACE

This traditional *sofra* is a design prevalent in the Eastern Mediterranean and can be found as far east as Bokhara in Uzbekistan. The mounds of cushions make it a perfect place to read a newspaper in the morning shade or to gaze at the stars on moonless nights. The white curtain leads to a passage that links my bedroom and sitting room.

105

A VIEW FROM the Sofra Terrace.
A jasmine frames the door, and rampant
plumbago tumbles over the low wall.
A miniature bonsai olive tree sits
alongside a pot of angel balm — a kind
of thyme — carried from England.

JS BEDROOM

The nineteenth-century bed is brass and painted metal, with classical motifs on the bedposts topped with brass finials. The white cotton curtains with crocheted hems were made some forty years ago. On the floor is a blue and white *dhurrie* from Jaipur. In the foreground is an Indian ivory sewing box. On the right is an older photograph of the room before the gilt lamp replaced the reading light now hidden at the back. There is a Greek breakfast of jam and biscuits, and a Chinese wicker basket to keep the tea hot.

JS BATHROOM

The trellis of the *mashrabiya* gave shade and privacy to the women of the harems of Constantinople, Cairo, and Damascus. Trellis work was typical of islands in the Dodecanese under Turkish domination for generations, but had died out on Patmos before I resuscitated it — it seems to have become mandatory in all houses now built or restored on the island. Turkish *hamam* towels, light and quick to dry, hang on the wall to the left. The trellised door hides a medicine cupboard. Old plates from Samos rest upon shelves painted sky-blue. On the right, a stone step leads to a large shower. On the parapet are a waffle towel and blue herringbone linen hand towel. The trellis partitions, allowing light and air to move freely through the room, have curtains made of cotton saris from Orissa in India. The JS-designed mirror is painted pistachio green. On either side, the brass bulkhead lights are in keeping with the bathroom's rusticity, as exemplified by the stone floor with whitewash in between.

112

JS SITTING ROOM

The low table (below) was painted by a local fisherman in a spontaneous naïve style. The plate depicting two fish is from the island of Skiros. The tables are stone and cement with wooden tops inspired by the refectories in the monasteries of Mount Athos. One is a double-sided writing desk and the other is a long, rectangular table for a computer and its accessories. The cotton *dhurrie*, always cool on bare feet, is from Rajasthan.

114

AT THE WRITING DESK, a Malcontenta chair designed by JS is
painted a shade of celestial blue. A detail of the window ledge
shows a stone head and other archaeological fragments from
the ancient civilizations that once surrounded Patmos —
treasures that have migrated indoors over the years. The white
stones are from Aspronisi, the island of dazzling white cliffs in
the Patmos archipelago.

LOOKING THROUGH to the breakfast terrace with the two-sided writing
desk in the foreground. The books have been chosen for their relevance to the
region — Greek poetry, travel essays, and studies of the Ottoman Empire by
Freya Stark and others.

Atop the bookcase is a brass jug used in milking a camel. A side table
holds a turquoise Venini lamp, a wooden statue of a Japanese samurai,
komboloi (worry beads) of amethyst, and blue ceramic and glass beads.
An eighteenth-century white ceramic jug from Este in the Veneto is used
for flowers. The plate is an M-D design; the cloth a blue and white Indonesian
ikat. So as not to distract from their chalky whiteness, the walls have been left
bare. The floor is terra-cotta, the last tiles made on the island in true old style.
Typical of Patmos is the door within a door, made by the local carpenter.

THE BREAKFAST TERRACE

The JS Malcontenta chairs are painted a bright shade of
terra-cotta and surround a table used for breakfast
or lunch in a part of the garden that always provides shade.
Behind the ferns and the elephantine leaves of the taro plant
Alocasia macrorrhiza is the *nosokomion* (hospital), where plants
are taken to recover in deepest shade.

121

122

AN ENORMOUS TARO plant and a fragrant gardenia sit under the dappled shade of a pergola. In early June, the spectacular amaryllis blooms in pots. The spiny, glaucous leaves of *Agave americana* contrast with the subtle green and white hues and softer form of a neighboring hydrangea. The multicolored flowers of the gray-leaved *Echeveria secunda* begin to emerge on stalks beneath the spiky, erect leaves of a yucca plant.

124

THE TOP OF THE BREAKFAST
TABLE is a mosaic of an octopus, a
creature of the sea delicious to eat
when boiled and sprinkled with
olive oil and parsley, or grilled on
charcoal. The surrounding motif of
waves recalls the gods of ancient
Greece that hover over the island.

A GUEST BEDROOM

The blue painted wooden four-poster bed has muslin
curtains that can be untied. The crocheted bedcover was
made with love and care by the present housekeeper's
grandmother. *Kilims* from Turkey cover the floor. On the
walls is a collection of Indian miniatures mounted on
traditional hand-printed fabrics from Rajasthan.

A VIEW FROM the guest bedroom. On the left is a small sofa painted *bois de rose* with JS-designed fabrics covering the cushions. Pink *hamam* towels are on a rack. A pot worthy of Ali Baba stands in the adjoining Moscoudi courtyard.

THE MOSCOUDI COURTYARD

An early-seventeenth-century pointed arch (the rounded arch came to Patmos later) leads to a courtyard of the old Moscoudi house, with bougainvillea and jasmine exploding overhead. Leading from it is a bathroom belonging to a guest bedroom. A red-striped canvas curtain covers a door leading to the labyrinth of winding streets that surrounds the monastery.

THE SECOND FLOOR IS ALSO A MAZE OF ROOMS.

THE TOP TERRACE IS REACHED by whitewashed stone steps to the side of the kitchen, leading from the entrance courtyard. A door leads into the sitting room, the painted anteroom, and a corridor whose walls have shelves crowded with photographs (there is also a hidden door that leads to the street). There is a bathroom for the guest bedroom, with a terrace and steps leading down to the Moscoudi courtyard. Parallel to this sitting room and adjacent to the White Room is the Turkish *Sofra* room and a small guest bedroom.

132

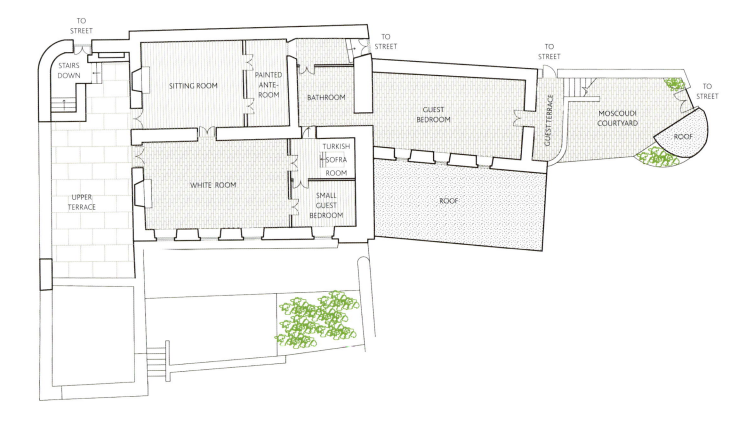

IN 1981 AN ADJOINING FARMHOUSE was purchased from the woman who had been the caretaker of its old and lonely owner, Mrs. Kyria Moscoudi. The two houses were joined, and a large painting studio on the second floor was made for Millington-Drake.

In the rooms, the Mediterranean that was the very center of the world awaits us: old kilims from Anatolia lie contentedly alongside bright dhurries newly commissioned from India;

THE GRAPEVINE shades the steps that lead down to the entrance courtyard.

an ornate brass and wood chest found in the Hadhramaut sits beneath a large eighteenth-century Italian mirror. Also finding a place in the quiet rooms are an inlaid ivory Moghul desk, rare Turkish embroideries, an ebony Italian chest, Indian miniatures mounted on antique Indian cottons, a Damascus chest set with mother-of-pearl, Venini blue glass, Saracen daggers, glinting Greek icons, white crochetwork made by the housekeeper's grandmother, Venetian gilt lanterns, English Regency letter boxes, and Samos pottery. Although few antiques were to be found on the island when Stefanidis arrived, the occasional portrait of a long-dead merchant frowns from the walls, and a small wedding chest with a motif of cypresses, bought years ago from an old Patmiote family, sits beneath a painting by Millington-Drake.

Everywhere there are recessed casements, the heavy carved wooden shutters offering relief from the noonday sun. From every window on the south side of the house, it is possible to see the small church of the Prophet Elijah, visible at the first moment of waking and throughout the long day, glistening in the sun atop its hill. From the upper terraces of the house, one sees past the large church of St. Mary the Saviour to the great monastery of St. John the Divine. The town of Chora, once home to the foreign workmen who came in the eleventh century to build the monastery, leans against the thick ramparts of the church and spills down the hillside in terraces. At night, the looming mass of the monastery hovers protectively above the town, while to the south, goats move across the dark fields, their faint rustling mingling with the melodic song of their bells.

THE UPPER-FLOOR TERRACE

The M-D drawing and photograph show the view of the
church of St. Mary the Saviour and the monastery above.
The blue-and-white-striped curtains protect the carved
doors from the sun. In the foreground, the folding
campaign chairs in white canvas are easy to carry and suit
the terrace as much as they do the African bush.

134

AS THE ORIGINAL TERRACE floor leaked badly — Patmiote tiles were no longer manufactured and modern tiles would have been strident — my solution was to have a cement floor divided in rectangles by small, black pebbles brought from a remote beach. The chapel of Prophet Elijah — the highest point of the island — can be clearly seen, and beyond it, the sea. The bench has mattress cushions in white canvas.

ABOVE: A view to the west.
RIGHT: A view to the garden,
and south and east to the sea.

THE UPPER-FLOOR SITTING ROOM

The ceilings in this room and in the White Room are over four meters high. A Millington-Drake watercolor shows a chest brought from the Hadramaut in South Yemen, and beyond it, a fern in a basket and a studded brass chest from Zanzibar. The door leads to the upper terrace. This detail shows the simplest of trestle tables, made on the island and used as a desk. The chair is early-eighteenth-century Anglo-Indian in ebony with a cane seat. The small chairs (shown on page 142) are also in ebony, and reminiscent of Jacobean style. The catches to close the shutters are characteristically Patmiote.

HARMONY CAN BE ACHIEVED by mixing designs and textures from diverse parts of the world. This room in Egyptian and Carmelite brown has tones of cream and dusty brown. The *kilims* possess the vibrant colors found in natural blue, red, and ochre dyes. The subject of the triptych by Teddy Millington-Drake is antique myths — the words depicted are Psyche, Eros and Love, Zeus, and Aphrodite, whose favorite island was Cyprus. Zephyros, god of the west wind, is often depicted as a handsome winged youth. The jumbo-sized island sofa was made for the room. On top of the bookcases on either side are sculptures by Gordon Baldwin and two watercolors — an abstract painting on the right and one of Easter Island statues on the left. The cushions of geometric design were woven in Africa. The windows above the doors, typical of Patmos, give light to the rooms beyond. Once used for sleeping, it is now the Painted Anteroom. I bought the early-eighteenth-century carved Tuscan mirror in Rome. The seat beneath is covered in hand-blocked fabrics from Rajasthan.

THE PAINTED
ANTEROOM

THE PAINTED ANTEROOM has maize-colored Japanese *tatami* matting on the floor; a blue and white cotton *dhurrie* from India in the center; a Turkish tray holding glasses; and a seventeenth-century large and strict Tuscan chair with gold foliate decoration, covered in an Indonesian *ikat*. The two trellis (*kafasoto*) cupboards were made on the island and painted a blue-green color — called Niagara in the nineteenth century. The walls were painted by Millington-Drake immediately after the house was bought, with images of the sun and moon. A Buddhist mantra takes up the wall above the drinks cupboard. A watercolour by M-D shows a view into the White Room and through the window to the ever-magical view of the chapel of the Prophet Elijah.

THE WHITE ROOM

This room has a sense of repose and purity. A stark room, it nevertheless has the sparkle of mother-of-pearl from a Syrian chest, a chair in the corner, and two small stands in the window. There is a glint of brass from low Indian tables, but other than that, nothing but white and nutmeg and copper brown. The mattress cushions and scatter cushions on the Empire-style sofas are all white, as are the covers of the ultra-comfortable chaise longues from the 1970s.

THE CENTER WINDOW in the White Room has a view of farmland
and the sea beyond. In one corner is a folding chair in Renaissance
style, inlaid with mother-of-pearl. As everywhere in the house
where there are tiles, the floor is edged with a band of whitewash
that soothes the eye — this has a practical purpose and hides the
drips when the walls are whitewashed each year.

THE TURKISH SOFRA ROOM AND SMALL GUEST BEDROOM

Looking through to the raised platform of the Turkish *Sofra* Room on the left and a guest bedroom on the right. The doors and windows dividing these rooms are glazed in blue glass. The high window has green, red, and blue glass panels. The wall hanging is Moroccan, with cushions in felt appliqué made on the island. All other cushions, including the mattress cushions, are in red and white striped cotton. The lamp, engraved metal in an old Topkapi design, is of waxed fabric, with loops that fold flat.

A SMALL MOROCCAN *eglomisé* mirror hangs on the wall. The door on the right leads to a guest bedroom that has an iron four-poster bed hung with hand-emboidered curtains from northern Greece, with pink grosgrain ribbons. The fringed and crocheted bedcover came from Malta.

THE MAIN GUEST BEDROOM

This room was once a studio, as is evident in the
photo showing Millington-Drake in a reflective
pose. On the right, a drawing of the same room,
which has since become the main guest bedroom.

159

THE ROOM ON page 158 is now a bedroom. Here the JS four-poster bed of wood, made on the island, is painted an ecru color also known as Dust of Paris. The bed curtains are released by untying the ribbons. In the foreground is a Japanese barber's chair in red lacquer. The floor is covered in a *kilim* and striped *dhurries*. Gouache and pencil drawings sit on a shelf above the door leading to a small, secluded terrace. The oil paintings in ochre, orange, and mastic brown are a salute to the previous occupant, Teddy Millington-Drake.

TWO OF THE THREE windows in the room overlook the *patelia* roof of
beaten clay, made in a timeworn method. The clay is excavated from the
island's quarries and flattened with wooden mallets until it proves
watertight. This traditional method needs to be done every autumn
before it starts to rain. Most of the roofs on the island are now made of
cement, which does not need this annual maintenance. Beyond the two
hanging curtains — one green, embroidered with brown flowers and a
brown fringe, and the other of red and white checks embroidered in
white with a fringe to match — is the guest bathroom.

IN THIS ROOM is a cornflower blue trellis cupboard (see page 162). Behind the M-D painted screen is additional hanging space. A planter's chair is covered in a terra-cotta cotton. The bookcase holds books on India and volumes of poetry. A Japanese candlestick, electrified and given a metal shade reminiscent of a coolie's hat, sits on a terra-cotta trellised table. The mirror is from Aleppo in Syria and has a rolling wooden panel to protect the glass. The small vase of Iraqi metalwork holds zinnias and scented pelargonium leaves from the garden. The back of the bed is hung with an ochre cotton sari from Benares. The traditional ceiling, using seaweed as insulation, has beams that alternate with sheaves of bamboo, similar to the ceiling in the Ithaka bedchamber of Odysseus and Penelope.

OVERLEAF:
The main guest
bedroom terrace.

164

PART THREE

GARDEN ROOMS AND TERRACES

BY SUSANNA MOORE

In the Middle Ages, it was believed that the seeds of all the plant species of the earth had,

like Eve, their origins in Eden [Dante, Purgatorio 28.109-20], a hypothesis that every

devoted human gardener is inclined to believe. ROBERT POGUE HARRISON

T HE DRY AND ROCKY LAND bought in 1964 (more land was bought in 1971, and again in 1981) falls in shallow terraces to a broad valley dotted with small white farmhouses. Across the valley is the stony hill crowned by the small chapel dedicated to the Prophet Elijah, built atop the ruins of a temple of Apollo. This gentle transition from terraced garden to yellow fields enclosed by low stone walls to rock outcroppings and barren hills makes for the tension Stefanidis believes is necessary in a created landscape. The alternation of light and shade, as well as wilderness and cultivation, straight lines and curves, aridity and verdancy allows — even requires — the incorporation of the world outside the garden. In Arabic, the word *al-jinnah* means both garden and concealment — a place of repose and a place of joy. To achieve this seamless yet defined vista, trees were cut down and trees were planted, walls were built and walls torn town, a dovecote was erected and an olive grove planted, all to direct the eye to the horizon dotted with the floating black shapes of distant islands. The order of the garden spills into the necessarily less ordered village and farmland surrounding it, and the great, mysterious world beyond.

Stefanidis remembers that in 1965, when rainwater was "collected in the winter on the roof and stored in large stone cisterns, the largest one beneath the entrance to the house, it

KEY

✻	CYPRESS
✿	OLIVES
❁	PINE
✳	PALM
⚘	CACTUS
⬡	EUCALYPTUS
✾	PRICKLY PEAR
❀	TREES
○	CERAMIC POTS
▦	WALL
◉	WELL
▨	PEBBLES
▩	STONE PAVING
▬	ROAD

was impossible to do much in the garden with its few old almond trees and dried-up citrus trees. Years later, when the local council installed a system that provided water for five hours a week, what had been unthinkable became possible — it was at last conceivable to begin to think of a small garden." In 1983, once the supply of water was sufficient, four dozen cypresses were planted, as well as the Lemon Terrace. The tumbled-down terraces were strengthened, and stone steps were laid. Small, fragrant bowers of shade were designed for reading or dozing, or for meeting friends in the evening.

On an unforgiving island, as more desperate times were replaced by days of good fortune, the garden was to be a refuge. The original garden had been kept to blue and white plantings, but Stefanidis brought black pelargonium, the uncommon variegated bougainvillea, and rare angel balm from his garden in Dorset. He planted every kind of basil, as well as milky green datura, glossy myrtle, scarlet and pink hibiscus, agapanthus, aloe, and gardenia. Because of the scarcity of water, Stefanidis decided to make a terrace of cacti, with accents of box, often

KEY

1 OUTSIDE DINING TERRACE
2 BUTTRESS TERRACE
3 JS SOFRA TERRACE
4 BREAKFAST TERRACE
5 FREYA STARK TERRACE
6 HERB GARDEN
7 PLUMBAGO TERRACE
8 LEMON TERRACE
9 FOUNTAIN TERRACE
10 CACTUS TERRACE
11 PRICKLY PEAR AND
   EUCALYPTUS TERRACES
12 TOMB GARDEN
13 CHAPEL
14 VEGETABLE GARDEN
15 DOVECOTE
16 OLIVE TERRACES

in pots. He scoured the nurseries of Athens for cacti, agave, and yucca, and distinctly Mediterranean plants such as *sarcococca*, and *teucrium* with its slate-blue flowers. Visits to the Botanical Garden in Rome, as well as to the Bronx Botanical Garden in New York, resulted in new plantings. A small and delicate carved marble fountain, found in India fifty years earlier by Millington-Drake's sister, Marie, was given its own terrace with *Westringia fructiosa* planted beneath olive trees, and an ailing almond tree was revived by a botanist from Kew.

Automatic watering, using a drip system, was installed on each terrace — an essential improvement from the days of water rationing. A stone dovecote with terra-cotta fanfares in a traditional design was inspired by the birdhouses on the Cycladic island of Tinos, and doves, at first cautious, came in flocks to live in it. An herb garden was made with coriander, mountain sage, parsley, arugula, mint, and lemon verbena. Hundreds of olive trees, as well as carob, grapefruit, lemon, orange, and palm trees, were planted on land leased to a local farmer for the traditional payment of one goat a year. The head gardener from the Chelsea Physic Garden in London visited to give advice, and helped train Theolougo, the gardener, to be fearless in his pruning. Pale stones from the beach were carried up the hill for the cactus garden, and even more palms, cypress, and pine were put into the lower fields. New whitewashed stone walls were built, snaking around the property. A small whitewashed tomb was built in memory of the late Teddy Millington-Drake, who died on the island. Depending on the time of day and the season, the paths of the garden soon led from fragrance to fragrance — rose, dianthus, lily, jasmine, gardenia, and the almost unbearably lovely *Cestrum nocturnum* or Queen of the Night. A friend has described the garden as "un giardino non costruito ma sognato." Not made, but dreamed.

⟨•⟩

For many years after the arrival of Millington-Drake and Stefanidis in the early 1960s (in 1966 a nearby house was bought and restored as a place for guests), and despite the consequent revival of local crafts and traditions, the island remained isolated in its glittering sea. Stefanidis remembers that a decade of profound stillness remained to them — no cars, no buses, no motorcycles, no electricity in the valley beneath the house, few shops, and no tourists (there is still no airport on Patmos, despite occasional attempts to build one). When cruise ships were in the harbor, visitors to the monastery had to climb the hill on donkeys. The first private telephones were not in use until the late 1970s, and it was only in 1971 that an American woman generously paid for the stifling monastery library to have air-conditioning.

A familiar superstition on the island is the evil eye. Children, donkeys, and old women wear the little blue bead in the shape of an eye to protect them from spite and covetous envy.

OPPOSITE:
TOP LEFT: A Judas tree (*Cercis siliquastrum*) in flower in April.
TOP RIGHT: A view from the garden to a distant chapel.
BOTTOM LEFT: Two ridged Patmiote terra-cotta pots.
BOTTOM RIGHT: *Solanum wenlandii* in full bloom.

TEDDY'S DRAWING shows an air-conditioner being lowered into the monastery by helicopter, a gift from a generous American lady.

A Millington-Drake
watercolor of the
steps descending to
the old garden.

A GARDEN I once had in the West Country in England possessed a different kind of sensuality, and one that suited a damper climate. The leaves of the walnut tree in that garden were pungent in the rain, as was the smell of grass, and the scent of old-fashioned roses that would have no chance of survival in the hot climate of an island in the eastern Mediterranean. My compensation has been waves of wafting jasmine and honeysuckle, verbena and rosemary, and the night-flowering jasmine (*Cestrum nocturnum*) aptly called Queen of the Night. The garden on this predominantly bare island is a cool refuge in the heat or after a wind-swept day spent at sea. Walking through the terraces to the olive grove, I am always reminded that Kalypso's island was also an enchanted garden.

It is considered very bad to compliment a mother on her child, or a farmer on his donkey, lest you incite ill fortune. This fear, first recorded by the ancient Greeks who used the amulet to protect themselves from the vengeance of Nemesis, is omnipresent throughout the Mediterranean. To avert the curse, one must turn aside one's head and spit three times while muttering the words, "May it not be blighted." It is a wish for the sacred island that has worked its spell.

Despite the inevitable encroachment of the modern world, some things have not changed. The legends of St. John remain vibrant on the island. A fisherman will readily point out the lovely bay where the evil sorcerer Kynops was transformed by St. John into an enormous rock, and there is a dark sea cave, believed to be the home of one of the more powerful devils of Patmos, that rings with strange and ominous cries when the tide is high. The Chapel of St. John at Sykamia still stands, in the fold of a hill, a few yards down a dusty path from the winding road from Chora to Grikou. Near the tiny whitewashed chapel and beneath a flourishing date palm is an old Roman bath, said to have been used by St. John to baptize Christians. It is one of hundreds of chapels, sheltering the hundreds of saints who protect the island. "The Aegean saint is not an object of contemplation; he is too present for that kind of reverence. His position is that of an ordinary human, except that he is in the fortunate position of liaison between God and man — more a Platonic *daemon*," Lawrence Durrell wrote, "than a simple saint." It is only right that the saints of Patmos should be half-human, standing as they do on the very pedestals of the ancient gods they have overthrown: gods whose moral qualities they have inherited. "The landscape puts her nymph's arms about human habits, beliefs, styles of mind so that imperceptibly they are overgrown by the fine net of her caresses — paths choked with weeds, wells blocked by a fallen coping-statue, fortresses silvered over with moss. Decay superimposes its own chaos, so that standing on some heap of stones today, watching a shepherd milk his goats, hearing the drizzle of milk in the cans chimed by the whiz of gnats which hover round him, you wonder whether this mauled assembly of stone is Frankish or Mycenean, Byzantine or Saracen. Often enough, the answer is: all of these."

FREYA STARK TERRACE

At the bottom of steep, narrow steps leading from the Buttress Terrace is a shaded terrace with a rough stone floor. A pergola was built in the 1960s, supported by thick whitewashed columns, to create a retreat in which to read and write. Freya Stark discovered this refuge during one of her visits and soon made it her own — it seemed fated to bear her name and has been known ever since as the Freya Stark Terrace. Her spirit suffuses the terrace, as made evident over the years by the numerous writers who have worked there each morning.

TOP LEFT: A view of the columns on the Freya Stark Terrace which were added at the very beginning of the house's renovation.
TOP RIGHT: The carved capital of a column surrounded by succulents.
BOTTOM LEFT: An Andre Dubreuil lamp on the wall of the terrace used for candlelit dinners.
BOTTOM RIGHT: A tray holding lunch.

178   ONE OF THE SIX outside rooms was named after Freya Stark, the venerated scholar who wrote about the Middle East and nearby Turkey. During her visits to the house, she would write on the terrace each morning before going for a swim and a picnic on the beach. A traditional Patmos sofa is painted black, as are the wicker armchairs covered in a royal blue fabric that will not fade in the sun. The four cement columns have been whitewashed so often they now bear a thick, chalky patina.

THE PLUMBAGO TERRACE
AND HERB GARDEN

Another place for drinks and a chat is the Plumbago Terrace, overhung by olive trees and majestic cypresses.

The herb garden opposite the terrace has raised beds for parsley, mint, coriander, thyme, and arugula. Lemon verbena (*Aloysia triphylla*) is used daily for making tea. Pots of white agapanthus and trailing pelargonium cascade in the shade of the olive trees.

181

THE LEMON TERRACE

Lemon trees, planted many years ago, give the terrace its name. As the original trees did not prosper, new lemon, orange, and grapefruit trees were planted in large pots. Pebbles from the island's beaches were used to make a floor. The island sofa is painted larkspur blue with canvas cushions of deep turquoise. The stone seat is long and wide enough to lie on, and a restful place to spend the morning. The small JS tables are painted blue, outlined in ruby red, turquoise, and navy, with pale blue feet. The JS lanterns are painted either sky blue or pistachio green. The JS Odessa chairs in pale celadon green are comfortable enough without cushions to be used for dinner at the round table at the far end of the terrace (see page 184).

THE FOUNTAIN TERRACE

At the end of a path, flanked by *Limonastrum monopetalum* mixed with various roses and circled by *Westringia fruticosa*, is a Moghul marble fountain of elegant simplicity. A more generous supply of water in recent times meant that the fountain could be used after years of storage. The marble plaque among the pebbles is a reminder that it was purchased by M-D's sister, Marie Paterno di Carcaci.

THE CACTUS TERRACE

From this terrace overlooking the Tomb Garden, you can see the chapel of St. George and St. Eustace. *Agave americana*, *Agave victoriae-reginae*, *Yucca aloifolia* "*Variegata*," *Dasyrilon acrotrichum*, and other succulents and cacti jostle for position among the round, gray stones that are a perfect foil to the army of prickly spines and fleshy spears.

188

THIS PATH edged by beds of cacti and succulents leads to the Eucalyptus Garden (not shown) and to steps leading down to the Tomb Garden, dovecote, and olive groves. The trunks of trees are traditionally painted white to protect them from insects.

THE TOMB GARDEN

A tomb of simple design by John Stefanidis is the center of the lower part of the garden. A stone path circumvents the chapel to lead to the dovecote and olive groves below. A small garden has sweeps of *Santolina chamaecyparissus* on each side of the path, olive trees with trunks painted white, and a grove of white oleander punctuated by dark green cypresses and palms. Soft clouds of trees are a contrast to the vegetation and serve as a windbreak when the *notus* or south wind blows.

TEDDY
MILLINGTON DRAKE
1932-1994
XAIPE

A MARBLE PLAQUE to
commemorate the late Teddy
Millington-Drake bears the
ancient Greek greeting, XAIPE.

THE CHAPEL OF ST. GEORGE AND ST. EUSTACE

On the street side of the garden (see plan) is a simple seventeenth-century chapel with buttresses that overlooks the olive groves. The iconostasis screen is beautifully decorated.

ABOVE LEFT: A bell tower is visible from the herb garden and terraces below.
ABOVE RIGHT: A modern icon of St. George slaying the dragon.
BELOW LEFT: A detail of the screen.
BELOW RIGHT: One of the two doors of the chapel leading into the courtyard with a gate to the street and a door into the garden above.

THE DOVECOTE

The progression of terraces led me to think that after a turn in the
Tomb Garden, and past the cistern and vegetable patch, there should
be a celebratory building — what better than a dovecote, modeled on
those of Tinos in the Cyclades. The doves swoop up and down, past the
chapel, the town of Chora, and the chapel of Prophet Elijah, and across
the distant bay of Grikou.

THE OLIVE TERRACES

There are eight terraces planted
with olive trees (*Olea europea*).
The walls and terraces were recently
rebuilt in Patmiote style with
triangular whitewashed coping.